THE UNKNOWN UNKNOWNS

THE UNKNOWN UNKNOWNS

Creativity, Arts and Ideasthesia

Vera Dragilyova

Verarta Books

CONTENTS

INTRODUCTION

Ideasthesia is a neurological phenomenon, where abstract thought is experienced in physical ways. It happens in the mind's eye of the thinker, but feels exactly like the physical reality we all know. Thoughts have size, weight, color, texture, velocity, smell, and all the attributes that any physical object we know. When the physical avatars of abstract thoughts interact, they emerge into shapes that provide answers. Just imagine throwing some chemicals together, only to get an explosion: that is exactly what Ideasthesia feels like!

Herself an Ideasthete, the author offers a whole slew of examples of ideasthetic thinking methods, in her book entitled "Ideasthesia." In this book, "The Unknown Unknowns", the reader is invited to follow along, as the author explores general creativity, literature, film, fine art, science, design and teaching,—treating them all as art, and arriving at surprising conclusions through ideasthetic thinking.

Just like mathematics is a code for describing the unseen laws of physical reality, ideasthetic thinking is a code for treating abstract thought: social and cultural processes, matters of the heart and soul, and the arts—anything that is hard to grasp without their analogue in the physical world. Ideasthetic thinking is really metaphoric, and as such, would make this book into a collection of drawings, if not translated into plain language. The material is presented as a collection of some practical and some philosophical observations on various topics, derived exclusively from ideasthetic thought.

There are questions to which we don't have answers: those are the known unknowns. Yet, there are ideas that lay beyond the horizon of any knowledge: those are answers for which we have yet no questions. According to the author, creativity is an ability to leap beyond this horizon, to what we yet don't know we don't know—the unknown unknowns—everything that we call art.

—Mr. Reed Wright

CREATIVITY.

"What am I doing? I am swimming in someone's qualia,"—thought Mr. Reed Wright.

Art and creativity.

We either fear the unknown or idealize it, but we don't expect it to be ordinary. Art is never ordinary, otherwise, it is no longer art. Art is the world of the unknown unknowns, accessible to humans only through creative spontaneous leaps of consciousness. No conscious effort can make one arrive in that mysterious land, and if it happens—it happens as suddenly and uncontrollably, as something one never thought of thinking, as if it thought itself into being.

Crabwork.

What is the opposite of creativity? Ladies and gentlemen: introducing to you the word crabwork. Neologism. Vague noun. Engagement in busy work that involves a great deal of entropy, with an exorbitant number of requirements, unclear scope, and usually dubious outcomes. Crabwork kills creativity, but it is what many people have to do, when they are ordered to be creative.

Divergent vs convergent thinking.

Creativity is divergent thinking: this is where one collects all ideas, without censure or judgement. Convergent thinking is anti-creativity, it is an editor, where one evaluates those ideas, sifting out the bad ones and keeping the good ones. This shift from divergent to convergent, and back to divergent thinking looks like a sinusoid curve, like a sound wave,—like a light wave. Interestingly, it is also roughly what in the field of

Artificial Intelligence is called Adversarial Networks. It is the divergent thinking that ventures into the unknown, which is the quintessential task of all creativity.

A known unknown.

A known unknown is something you have grasped with your mind from the outsider, like a black box with a mystery inside. You can see the negative space that the boundaries of your knowledge create, and this negative space marks the territory of the unknown. An unknown unknown is something you have yet to notice and then surround with your mind, and then get inside, to know it completely. We will never know whether the unknown unknowns are even there or not, if we still don't know to even ask that question. When we find them by chance, there is no way to know whether they were there all along. Shroedinger's cat is miauing here all along! I think, our knowledge has no influence of the existence of the unknown unknowns. To us, they might appear like a creation, because they did not exist previously in our limited universe.

Art in physical terms.

If you were to visualize knowledge, it would probably look like a giant atomic mushroom, sprouting into space, like the universe expanding itself into nothingness, creating the unknown unknown.

Creating a work of art is answering a question you did not even know to ask. The unknown unknown is exactly like being dead—you would not know anything about the life you were missing. You could not even wonder about it. The only question you could ask is: what is it that I don't know about? It is exactly like not living in some faraway country right now and not missing anything about it—you would not even know what to miss. Yet, that country is there, right now, and you are missing out. In fact, there are billions gazillions of places and events in many countries on which you are missing out right this second, and you would never know to think about it. This is how the world of creativity feels!

Input, processor, output.

We can look at creativity in a mechanical way, too. It takes a deep, emotional, thoughtful, and intellectually developed person to create something extraordinary, and there are three essential parts in the process of creation: the input, the processor, and the output. Roughly speaking, input is life experiences, processor is the mind, and the output is the resulting work of art.

The input is the summation of life experiences of a person. Actors are known to win their Oscar after a traumatic event in their lives, so are artists, musicians, writers, and other creators—are known to produce their best work during or after some traumatic events. Maybe an average person would brush them off and move on, but the processor of a creative person gains its artistic energy in the depth of experience and pours it into the work of art it creates. The more far-reaching, complex and variegated an experience is, the more energy is mastered, and the greater the output, for a creative person. For others—it is just a hindrance, a distraction, a setback. Travel, which exposes one to new world views, smells, tastes, ideas and images, is one of the best ways to build complexity of one's life experience. Reading books and living parallel lives through its characters is also powerful.

Hyperactivity of the processor is a categorical imperative, sine qua non. The process of creativity looks like white noise—a cloud of stochastic trials and errors, or reshuffling patterns, some of which fall apart, dissipate into entropy, and are then recycled, and some of which persist. The more sensitive the processor, the more concrete ideas it will glean from the white noise, and the less entropy will be generated.

Sensitivity is a great predictive measure of one's creative potential. Even the smallest occasion will make a highly creative processor suffer intensely. It notices the most minute of details and dwells on them, re-living them many times over, in various re-combinations.

However, even the most extraordinary processor that is exposed to the most extraordinary experiences may not result is a work of extraordinary creativity. The output is in the ability to edify one's vision, which is the craft—not art!—side of creation. What one must have boiling and pressing from the inside, like a volcano,

threatening to come out, if no natural outlet is found,—
has to be shaped into a communicable output that others
can understand. It is an art in itself.

Mindfulness.

Very often, creativity is sparked by random
circumstances. Creation is largely about recognition and
awareness; otherwise, who knows what genius work of
art our mind might have created, if we are not aware of
it?

A hundred people will walk across a forest
path. Only ten of them will notice the flowers, thrown
haphazardly on the side of the road. Only five of them
will notice the girl who dropped them. Only two of
them will have noticed her tears. Yet, only one of them
will notice the beauty in the pattern of how the flowers
are lain, and remark that their color is of the lips of that
girl, and notice that the rain has started falling, in unison
with her tears, and a smiled whispered on her lips.
Statistically, even fewer than one person per hundred will
have imagined the story that has led to this remarkable
moment. What we do not notice—simply does not exist

for us. And the fewer details exist inside our mind, the fewer we have to play with, in order to create something.

Yes, having one's brain be hyper-open to the world can feel overwhelming. To those who experience such a bombardment of stimuli, daydreaming, getting away into the zone, is indispensable. Creativity demands sacrifices, and in this sense, it is the opposite of efficiency, streamlining, and often—opposite of clarity and peace.

Negating a form.

When evaluating any work of art, it is important to establish what it is doing: playing by the rules, negating an existing form, or creating something completely new? Negating a certain form for the sake of a sensation-driven negation is distractive, short-lived, and ideologically parasitic. Negating a form can be like throwing away the whole game because one does not like the rules. Instead of seeing the rules as a prison for free thought, they can be seen as a challenge, a springboard for imagination. It is the same as when a politician points to trivial problems in a society in order to distract public attention from his or her lack of good work. It can also be playful, but it is very often abused, for the lack of creativity.

Imprisoned imagination.

The fear of the unknown is the antithesis of imagination, while imagination is what humans have in common with God. The awe at the unknown is what sparks creativity.

We live lives of fictional freedom, starting with our bodies, which we cannot escape, with all their aches and pains, and sensitivities. Then, it is our clothes that constantly pressure, rub, and squeeze our flesh, in all the unnatural ways. Ah, and that heavy unescapable arm of gravity, weighing us down like shackles, incessantly strapping every cell of ours to the ground, when all we really want is to soar far and high into the sky—wild, relentless, and untethered. Then, it is our mind that plays a prison guard who, out of fear to get hurt, tells us what to think and what decisions to make, further tightening our tunnel vision. Even our heart whispers to us what to feel and forces us to pine for people who do not deserve us, despite our better judgement.

We barely look at the sky long enough to see how clouds move, we barely ever hold our breath at sunrise or sunset, to consciously register the incremental changes in the intensity and color of sunlight. All of it around us is alive and breathing, yet we spend most of our lives insulated ourselves from it, cocooned in the cell within a cell, within a cell, in a high security prison of self, as if its sole purpose was to protect us from life itself.

Wait, there is another layer. We movement through space is so limited, yet we take no notice. For example, we don't usually jump to the other side of the planet to peak on how someone is doing their thing, nor do we try to escape Earth's atmosphere to visit the Moon for the afternoon, to see how the craters are doing. That's physically impossible, and we know it. Even if a machine could take us there—we would have to pay for it. And in order to pay, we would have to be a part of the system that would dictate the terms of exchange of our energy and effort for the monetary units that would buy us out of our physical limitations —and take us where we want. Then, even if we get enough of those units to pay your way—to get to some places, you still might need a visa.

There will always be that un-seen lonely flower in the middle of the un-walked winding path in a beautiful forest that will wait for you all of infinity, except you will never even know. There will always be a million people that you never met and never will, there will always be a million chances that you could have taken but didn't, a million versions of your live you could have lived but didn't, and a million thoughts and feelings that you could have experienced but didn't, simply because you are a mere mortal, with all of the limitations that come with the title.

And we keep on living, the obedient servants of reality, dragging on this complacent existence, in a rational and fully justified denial of how imprisoned we are. We simply know no different and are so used to it— it is just easier to carry on. Our old imperfect ways have served us well enough, our theories of life are good enough to continue to tomorrow, we could always buy a smoother fabric that would feel good on the skin, and the state borders are so far away— we won't even know that they are there.

Yet, now and then, there is that recurring little itch, that underhanded alarm that rings through our mind, telling us that we want more and know that there is more there. We catch a whiff of temptation for a prison break, and it lingers in our noses even as we sleep. We ponder the question, until our brain gets callouses from walking us through the same vicious cycles of thought. There must be a way out. Where is our free will, when all we have is shackles and tethers, and limitations, all around us and all through us? We finally arrive at a eureka moment that changes us forever: the only escape, the thing that could set us free—is our imagination.

CREATOR'S BLOCK

"I am a bloke with a Writer's Block,"—thought Mr. Reed Wright.

Ideasthetic thinking allows me to create a physical model of abstract thought in my brain, where ideas come together, interact, and form into a result the answer. When I ask my brain what causes creativity blockage, or creator's block, I can see many factors merging together, like chemicals, with explosions, mutual annihilation, growth, and all kinds of other permutations. Probably, every human thinks in this way, but it remain in the subconscious. I actually see and feel this process physically, and the resulting answers are crystal clear. Here is what my brain tells me.

The way science is practiced in our modern society discourages imagination and creativity. Even before any ideas arrive, one is concerned about an ability to prove them: unproven ideas have little value. Why? Maybe because there are too many of them, and too many good ones are buried in the charlatanic morass, being equated and disregarded along with them. Calling unproven ideas hypotheses endows them with a social status and gives them some credence, but still.

The ancients had no such problems: they were all philosophers, and as such, had the right to cultivate claims a priori, using only the little stipulated logic that was agreed upon in those ancient times. Then, the world population was smaller, the competition was not much, and there was relatively little chance of reinventing the wheel, and so little possibility of plagiarism. Unbridled, new ideas blossomed.

Modern times are different: there are so many ideas under the sun, and we are worried more about plagiarism than about coming up with something new. Ideas are monetized, which means that they are up for grabs, spurious or not, and are attractive to any and all interested in profit. That attracts more money-mongers into the mix than actual genius inventors, inundating the space with so much abusive content that true treasures have a little chance of surviving the sheer social pressure. Then, there is politics involved, and competition is not based on merit anymore, but on one's will to power, while the truth has become stipulated and not deduced or discovered. Thus, many creators are nipping their creative process at the bud by cutting its air supply and burdening its wings with a weight all too heavy to lift off the ground, despite the overall social call for innovation.

The best ideas happen naturally, motivated by curiosity and wonder, and without fear or concern for any proof or practicality. The main barrier of invention in the modern world is this complex fear of what to do with the ideas, once they are born, and so ideas stay dormant within us.

Once we learn how to divorce ourselves from the quagmire of utilitarian thought, we can venture into freedom, where our whole being will be prepared to set itself free and create without bias. In addition to this paradigm shift, there are specific things one can do, in order to break the Creator's Block.

Pleasure.

Find anything that makes you feel good, happy, joyous, excited, and wholeheartedly focus on it. Then, come back to what you were working on, and see creative miracles happen. What makes us stressed and depressed, also makes us less creative. The reverse of that—pleasure—is manna for our creativity, when we are stuck in the desert. Feeling good relaxes the micro-manager, control freak part of our brain, and allows our thoughts to flow freely. Brainstorming in a relaxed, uncontrolled state is impossible without pleasure of some kind. Creative energy accumulates via pleasure.

Stress.

Stress kills creativity, through many processes, one of them—by activating the fight and flight response, which automatically blocks it. Stress makes us narrow our vision, so that we can focus on the source of stress,

—which is exactly opposite of open-mindedness necessary for creativity. If you are not able to create, check your stress levels, and relax, but don't try too hard —it is counterproductive. Do it gently and slowly, in increments.

You could be trying too hard, you could be simply too focused on something to engage in divergent thinking, and all your thoughts are being cut short, eliminated, and shortcut to simplify them— automatically.

Falling in love is certainly a stress for one's mind, but it can either stimulate creativity or stifle it. At the apex of problematic love, it becomes a stifling stress, and creativity is brought to a minimum, as one is either frozen in fear of a loss or is agonizing over it. It happens even when love is not problematic, but just extremely intense: it also stifles creativity, allowing it in only when things calm down a little. This is the reason people often claim that to be productive, one must stay away from intense romantic relationships. However, loss of creativity has to do with being in a love crisis, rather than in love in general. Some romantic excitement stimulates creativity, and a complete lack of it can lead to lethargy.

Being creative in the absence of love is only a sublimation, a re-channeling one's energy into creativity.

It is important to avoid repressing one's feelings, which make stress become chronic, and fossilized in our memories into gallstones that will have to be surgically removed one day. It is a painful procedure, yet preventable, if you are not afraid to face your fears. Your stress could be hidden, just under your conscious radar, so check yourself thoroughly, eliminate the source of it, and then, if nothing else is a culprit, creativity should be reestablished.

Depression.

When someone is depressed, their mental viewfinder is not just narrowed, like it is under stress, but it is reduced to a single dot—the tiny light at the end of the tunnel. Depression is a state of extreme focus on the feeling that tries to resolve the cause: thus circular and obsessive thoughts. Our brain is doing the opposite of free association, because it is working hard on eliminating the source of depressing by working it out on its own, a priori. You can help your brain by digging deep and search far and wide, to find the source of depression and eliminating it. Until then, it will be hard to tap into your natural creativity, because our mental resources are unavailable, busy with problem-solving and survival.

Maslow's Hierarchy of Needs.

When people are worried about basics in life, such as job security, paying bills, health, relationships, their creativity is naturally suppressed, as an adaptation mechanism to survive and overcome whatever is seen as most urgent by the brain. So, how is it that some very poor people are extremely creative? Different people have different thresholds of satisfaction, different expectations and standards. To some, a little something to eat is good enough, and they are no longer worried. Some are so engulfed by their process of creation that they forget to eat! Yet, no one can be creative, if they are too busy with survival—at the level that their individual brain dictates.

Tough love.

Have you ever wondered why some children wither down into wallflowers with some teachers, and blossom into creative geniuses with others? One of the reasons is the level of domination that each child needs, in order to be optimally creative. Everyone has a different starting potential, but the higher it is, the more sensitive a child is, and the less tough love and domination their creativity tolerates.

Adults, just like children, react to domination with either rebellion or with dejection, neither of which sparks imagination or helps creativity. Touch love can only curb certain behaviors, but it cannot inspire. The more tough love is involved, the more domineering and authoritative the order is, the less creative a truly creative person becomes. Inspiration has not a tinge of authority in it, and it is what one needs—not the stick, but the carrot,—in the form of something that will whet one's intellectual appetite or pique one's curiosity, or touch one's heart with its beauty.

Playfulness.

At the core of creativity is playfulness. It is an absolute lack of fear to try something new, complete nonchalance, complete engagement into the game of the discovering the unknown unknowns, whatever the price. It is a mindset of an adventurer: no fear and all excitement. Try putting yourself into this mindset, and creativity will not make you wait for long.

Relaxation.

Being able to relax is art, so fine and imperceptible is the line between coercing yourself to relax and naturally relaxing, the line that makes all the difference. You cannot try too hard to relax: it is counterproductive. The trick to relaxing is not trying anything, as in trying nothing at all. Any effort whatsoever will not allow your brain to relax. Not trying to think or create, not trying to meditate, not trying to stop worrying. Just trying nothing at all is the first step to relaxation, and it is necessary, before creation can begin.

Curiosity.

Few things will spurt your mind into agitated thinking like a good question. Human brain needs questions, mysteries, puzzles, so that it would use its excitement instinct and go for the chase. If stuck, find questions about your topic, look for what is still unknown, and your brain will do the searching and creating on its own. If you cannot find any questions, let any random stranger come up with one. Sometimes strangers have a much fresher and clearer vision of our topic, which allows them to get us unstuck from the mental route we have traced over and over in a vicious circle.

Stimulation.

Creating in isolation can be very productive, or very unproductive. What's the secret? It is about the golden middle, the apex of the Gaussian curve of how much stimulation your brain needs. Too little stimulation —and you are starving for the material to create. Too much stimulation—and you are overwhelmed, disorganized, and discombobulated.

Some people seek out solicitude and tranquility, in order to calm their thoughts, because they have too many as it is, and need to minimized external stimuli. That way, they can give them space for free association and clarity. That is creativity!

Other people don't have enough thoughts, are stuck in a usual futile pattern of thinking, feel antsy, and need the external world to wake them up, or to displace them from the repetitive thoughts with dead ends. They seek people, noise, music, and commotion, as those stimulate them up to an optimal level. Searching out the right amount and type of stimulation for each individual is crucial for inciting creativity.

Change of focus.

Creator's Block can sometimes be overcome by radically changing your activity, and engaging in something that will drive your thoughts to flow divergently. It is especially helpful when this activity is unfamiliar: that instantly activates and freshens up the brain, opening it up for restructure. Some examples of activities that have worked for me are: watching a film, listening to exhilarating music, meeting new exciting people, traveling to unfamiliar places, taking a long shower, and learning a difficult foreign language. It has to be something that sways you emotionally: emotion is a fundamental and indispensable driver of creativity. Even simple activities such as mindful walking in nature, driving, or making love are extremely powerful in freeing up imagination. They force the human brain out of focus, in order to open up its clutches over its own course of thinking, so that creativity can be unleashed. Finally, any physical activity, where strain is necessary, followed by an endorphin rush afterwards, is a great tool.

Slash and burn.

Some Creator's Blocks are so deep and stubborn that the only technique that works is what I call slash and burn. It is essentially extreme change of focus, and is a drastic measure. One has to put themselves into a situation that will pump adrenaline into your blood. I am not recommending anything life-threatening, but things that only seem to be threatening, like a scary ride in Universal Studios, or jumping off with a parachute. Anything that is going to wake up your whole being, safely. At the moment of its happening, creativity will not return, but it is more likely to return later, once you calm down.

Clutter vs organization.

Some people need what they call creative clutter to stimulate their creativity, saying that sterile environments are something that kills their ideas. Two things could be going on, and I clearly see them in my knots of ideasthetic thoughts. Firstly, when something looks barren, it appeals to the same emotion as loneliness, which in turn makes us feel stress and depression, thus stifling creativity.

Secondly, sterile environments rob the eye of visual stimulation that occur in nature: the patterns of leaves, branches, clouds, the foot paths in the forest, the sea waves, and the curves of sand dunes. They are all curvy and relatively un-uniform and unpredictable, which visually poses questions to the brain, and thus stimulates creativity.

On the other hand, such complex environments can feel like clutter to the brain: confusing, disorienting, distracting, and defocusing. Sometimes, when one has too many ideas, they turn into senseless white noise, very much like an orchestra dividing into ten parts, and each of the sections playing a different symphony. In this case, structure is needed, in order to simplify and clarify things, so that creativity can take place. In this case, cleaning up physical and emotional mess really helps, just as writing down one's thoughts in a form of a diagram or a list.

The tag of war between clutter and organization is fundamentally all about the right type and level of stimulation necessary for creativity.

Multitasking.

Multitasking is a type of stimulation, which can be too much for the brain, or it may move it to a higher level or alertness. More often than not, however, multitasking can feel dangerous, irritating, and distracting to the brain, and the brain will block off all extraneous creative thought, to focus all its resources on switching tasks efficiently.

Quantum Observer Effect.

The observer effect from quantum mechanics works the same in creativity. Observation alters intention, focus, and motivation. Creating under observation is like loving by force, where the process of creation becomes a process of dictation. The judgement inherent in observation, whether in the form of criticism or admiration, contaminates the very vacuum bubble of safety and freedom that surrounds creativity.

On the other hand, it works wonders, when the observer is the intended audience, and the creator is a performer. That kind of a relationship has to be agree upon, for the creativity to prosper.

Motivation.

Internal motivation, consisting of aesthetic, moral, or intellectual pleasure, is what determines creative success. What one notices, the associations one makes, and the types of answers one seeks out subconsciously—is all selected and directed by motivation. External motivations, consisting of things like money, public acceptance, or catering to someone else's standards that conflict with yours,—are sure to stifle the best of geniuses.

However, nothing can meddle with your creativity, if your motivation is to divulge and share your vision of the world, because its beauty presses you from the inside so much that you are about to explode,—then that guiding principle will let you create the best you ever could. If you follow anything else, you cut your chances at the bud. The main question is: how desperate is your need to express yourself? How much creative energy are you storing inside?

Tautology trap.

When, instead of creating new growth in one's work, one starts drawing their ideas exclusively from their own work, over and over again, we get tautology as a result. This is a common and convenient unconscious trap that eventually becomes a habit, and ultimately fails and convinces the thinker that they are simply not creative enough. Yet, it is only a method that can be changed! Detracting one's attention away from one's work and maximizing the breadth of one's life's experiences is a simple solution to this seemingly complex and cryptic problem.

Open vs closed spaces.

The Prospect-Refuge theory in Architecture tells us how being in open and closed spaces influences the mental state of a person, and this theory is certainly relevant in creativity. For extraverts, large windows with vast views, high ceilings, and big size rooms tend to inspire creativity and imagination. On the other hand, small spaces can make one feel claustrophobic, stifled and uninspired, which works similar to stimulation in general.

On the other hand, introverts may feel cozier, more relaxed, and more creative in closed environments. Little niches of safety may stimulate introverts to open up and create more freely. It is all about trying different options and discovering what works for each individual, very gently and without any prejudice.

The good news.

The fear of not being original, of not saying anything new or of significance can sometimes stifle creativity. The good news is that there will always be something new that no one has thought of before. It is because, statistically, there are more thought combinations possible than there are particles in the universe!

STORYTELLING

"Writing is like eating, but in the opposite direction,"—said Mr. Reed Wright.

Every story follows a trajectory of a heartbeat. A story is a cut-out from life: we cut out the clutter to focus on the form that instinctually feels complete, anticipating our curiosity. A story is not something we create, but it is something we discover and choose to tell.

In telling a story, we cut out the clutter to focus on the form that instinctually feels complete, just like Michelangelo chiseled away the extra pieces, in order "to find the angel inside." Yet, if we cut away too much, we can kill it. There is a golden middle of not revealing too little or too much, not only so that the story is clear, but that there is always an element of mystery that keeps the readers curious for what is to come next.

In my brain, every story is a film that creates and plays itself out, completely outside of my control. I watch it, and then hurry to write it all down, catching on to every detail. Curiously, a story is not a continuous sequence of events, but a selection of bits and pieces that make sense only in relation to each other. Curiously, this is also the reason we understand modern poetry and songs, where concepts seem to be simply thrown together, without any proper grammatical or even semantic connections. Grammar is really not necessary for comprehension, it turns out. Being at a loss for words does not mean being at a loss for thoughts!

Story structure.

A story structure without a story is barren. A story created to fit a structure—is dead. The world of the story already exists, waiting to be discovered, only pieces of it selected and recounted through a universal story structure, without having to distort the story itself.

Superimposed structure will look for the truth in its minutia of events, but in doing so—will annihilate the meaning. Only the structure that is discovered in the story can bring out the meaning and speak truthfully.

The structure of a story is a universal structure that looks like a Gaussian curve, paramount in nature, as well as in social and emotional processes. Even the sexual act follows the structure of a story! It is all about building pressure and then releasing it. Just like in lovemaking, a story is a series of calls and responses, of actions and reactions. There are two parallel call-and-response strings that follow a story: one is between the story and the readers, and the other one is between the protagonist and the antagonist, or the good and the bad, of the story.

How does the readers know who is who? The story is always told from the point of view of the protagonist, because whoever POV this is—becomes the protagonist. Any personage, from whose point of view the film is established as primary—automatically becomes a protagonist, even if they are extremely bad: thus the anti-hero. It is because that POV is de facto the self of the story, and humans are used to experience the world via self. An antagonist point of view is shown from the outside, so as to create an us-them dichotomy, prodding the readers to take sides and rood for their team—the protagonist.

Control and happy endings.

Reading a story feels exactly like being a passenger in someone's car, feeling that the driver is out of control. In fact, it is the passenger who is out of control, and so they find that the driving is unpredictable and dangerous. Once the readers take sides, they have an urge to control what happens to the characters. In fact, a story is not about what the main character wants. A story is about what the viewer wants to happen in the story. As a rule, the reader wants to solve the main problem, as well as all other problems on the way of the character for whom they root.

For a storyteller, delaying the desired action increases the reader's feeling out of control and their emotional effort to make the story go their way. Finally, when the desired action takes place, the reader exhales in an ecstasy of catharsis, and once again feel in control.

Being temporary out of control is exciting, and when the outcome is what the readers desire, they are highly satisfied.

This is why everybody loves good endings! It confirms that the reader is in control. In fact, a story is not over until there is a good note to end it on. It is because, at least, in modern times, a story is about overcoming hardships: if they are not overcome, one has not told everything there is to tell. If the characters fail, then this is a story not worth telling.

The reason people love stories is because they enjoy the process of dealing with the challenges and hardships, knowing that the result is good. Any story is the know-how, a boot camp, of how do survive, what to do, in order to come out victorious. A tragic story, on the other hand, teaches us what not to do, and is de facto incomplete. It is as if the story did not tell all the truth. And, in fact, it didn't: in addition to warnings, it should have taught us what should have been done: this is what everyone is waiting for. This is why, without a good ending, a story is incomplete, at least, in modern understanding. If it ain't good, it ain't over!

Justice and catharsis.

People like to see justice being served. No story is over in the mind of the reader, until everyone gets what they deserve. Sometimes, the whole story arc of a character is about transformation they deserve: from riches to rags, and from rags to riches. However, for the readers, all actions need justified reactions from the world of the story. There is a good reason why Cinderella story is timeless.

Even small acts of injury or injustice without a response cause frustration. For example, when a helpless child is beaten by a bully, the readers will want to punish the abuser. If the punishment is delayed, the intensity rises, and when punishment happens, the readers are satisfied. When someone deserves a punished for something and they don't get it, we walk away from the story with a lingering sense of frustration. We might even lose faith in humanity, and fall into lethargy, if we take things to heart.

Every story is like a court hearing: the readers must know who is guilty of what, then punishment must be served. Not having justice served makes the readers feel out of control and dissatisfied. It is all really about checks and balances, where the scales of good and evil must be even: an eye for an eye. It is justice that serves as a foundation of the overall cathartic experience.

By the way, the best trial lawyers are the best storytellers. Without a story, the application of laws loses all orientation, and judgements of who is bad and who is good—are impossible. The jury will only believe a story that rings true. It does not actually have to be true, but it has to be believable, one that harkens back to personal experience of individuals comprising the jury. How unjust! This is how powerful stories are: they make and break everything in the world of humans.

FILM

"Set a match on fire, then watch the whole world burn,"— *thought to himself Mr. Reed Wright.*

Films are exactly like dreams, in that they are comprised of only bits and pieces of visions and sounds, woven into a collage on a timeline, where the dreamer fills in the blank spaces. It is also very much like human eye movement and vision—naturally fragmented and collage-like. The meaning of a film is all in the relationship of its parts to each other, and there isn't an ending without a beginning and a middle, there is no culmination without an original problem, there is no protagonist without an antagonist. There is even no grey without white.

Directionality.

What moves these bits and pieces forward is a question, a hook of curiosity of what is to happen next: in this way, films are unidirectional. But are they? Some films offer us mental flashbacks, when the meaning is explained in retrospect, like connecting the dots in all directions for ultimate understanding. Some films envision the future, then return back to present to give it meaning. Watching a film the second time around completes the puzzle. In this way, to be fully understood, a film must be experienced as a collage of still images, where one all the images, all at once.

Complexity of rules.

The more meaningfully complex a film is, the more complex must be its internal rules, which serve as a reference system for understanding the meaning. The rules are gleaned from the inner world of the film, through uniformity that repeats itself. Lighting, plot, acting, photography rules—are all established with the first frames, really. That is why it takes only a few seconds for someone to get the mood of the film, and whether one will like it—it is all about tacit rules that one instantly perceives. The more fully the audience can perceive the rules, the more fulfilling the viewing experience will become.

Acting.

I have watched the highest-acclaimed actors in action, and I have realized certain qualities they have in common. They are: cultivating and enriching the self, then, like water, fitting this accumulated richness of character into the circumstances, and reacting to what is happening instead of acting ahead preemptively. This way, the acting does not feel contrived.

This is how a horoscope: the Barnum Effect! While the actor does not significantly change their facial expression, the viewers will read in the emotion, appropriate to the situation. Likewise, with any horoscope, a reader will relate to the description, regardless of their actual situation, by picking out parts that resonate, and interpreting them according to how they see fit their situation. The description does not change, but the interpretation from person to person—does drastically. With great actors, their acting does not change much, but audience perception of it does drastically, according to the circumstances. The presence of rich character in itself does the magic, and the film is judged as meaningful and touching, on the mere basis of its presence. This is why great actors can command large compensation—their rich character immediately endows any film with depth, context, and meaning.

Negative tendencies.

The problem with some of films in the recent mass market is their fetishism—their obsession with form and structure, without understanding the purpose they serve. Monetized movies attract superficiality in execution. Like bright waxed fruit with no aroma or flavor, such films are believed to make a better sell, if they follow certain formulas. However, formulas get old and overused, riding the wave of the original invention that inevitably peters down to nothing. The formulas are in plot, in acting, and even in themes that the films addresses. Yet, with time, plots become predictable, acting becomes unoriginal, and themes become overused. As a reaction to the obviously falling empire of copycats, a search for original unique ideas has surged, and it is an extremely good news!

What the best films have in common.

Depth of meaning has always won over the form that is devoid of it. There are four aspects that I have noticed to be present in all films that have proven successful in all of history, of all countries in the world. They are the following: Truth, Goodness, Vulnerability, and Unpredictability. All great films I have watched have those in common:

1. **Truth.** A film must ring true, in the plot itself, in the dialogue, in the decorations, and in everything else. Even a phantasy has to have motivated and plausible events. Everything has to be believable, in order to resonate with the viewer. Anything fake immediately disconnects the viewer from the magic of the experience.

2.   **Goodness.** There has to be a higher good that will touch the soul of the viewer. The film's theme, as well as the goals of the protagonist must be inspirational, objectively good, and appeal to the highest of moral values. Otherwise, the film will appeal to a limited audience.

3.   **Vulnerability.** Somehow, we humans, are wired to be good, to save, to protect, to stand up for the good. We all have a parental instinct that is activated when a character shows their vulnerable side. Our sense of justice is satisfied when a bad person is punished, making them vulnerable, as well as when an originally vulnerable underprivileged person gets ahead in the story. We even forgive the evil, as long as it is punished first, and becomes vulnerable. We forgive everything and we love wholeheartedly for one's vulnerability. Viewers find vulnerability irresistible, and there is barely any story possible without it. Having an invincible character is attractive, but without a vulnerable side, full connection is impossible. This reminds me of having salt and sugar in a cookie—it is the same in a

film. Any superior quality, if not softened by vulnerability, just becomes empty, repetitive, and tasteless.

4. **Unpredictability.** This is all about hooks and curiosity, being out of control, then regaining it, being addicted to suspense and surprises, about surviving and winning in surprising ways. Making the audience laugh, which is almost a requirement in any modern film, is caused by a surprise and is considered a stressor by the body of the viewer. Although it appears to be a reaction of joy, laughter is a nervous reaction, and crying is a reaction to an intense a stressor that laughter cannot handle. The release of endorphins in laughter makes a film addictive, while anticipating the unpredictable causes the release of adrenaline, which also ensures an addictive experience.

All four of these aspects are subconsciously used as reference systems by an audience—to judge the quality of a film. A cherry on top would be elements of nostalgia caused by a loss of something good and dear.

Moral accounting.

Viewers look for overall moral balance in the credits and debits of a film. Justice must be served one way or another, sooner or later, within the framework of a single story. If not—then a sequel is necessary, in hopes that it will fix it. That is one of main tools for continuation of a movie series. The balance is sought in answering the unanswered questions, in avenging the victims and punishing the evil-doers, the good-doers must get rewarded, the sufferers—assuaged, the lost must be found, debts must be repaid, and even the characters' actions must be justified.

A film can push and pull in different directions to destabilize the ethical balance in a plot, but that balance must be established, and the accounting of values must be matched in the end, if people are to walk away satisfied. It is the eternal fight between the good and evil, and it is even better when the good character, in the end, gets a little more than they expected, as long as it is exactly what they deserve. That way, they are repaid not only for the original wrongdoing done to them, but also for the time they waited for the balance to be reestablished, and for all the suffering their journey must have caused them.

Not giving viewers the satisfaction of a final balance is like playing a 7-tone scale and stopping at the 6th tone—it is excruciatingly painful and dissatisfactory. On the other hand, establishing final balance of moral values is what causes the viewer to experience catharsis and release at the end, by making whatever the outcome to appear as a happy ending in their eyes.

There are several moral conditions that make a film more satisfying to watch:

1. **High stakes, intense characters.** The film is most exciting when the stakes are maximally high: when the potential strength of both the protagonist and antagonist is highest, as they fight each other, and there is maximum of potential loss for each side. So, let's say, the values of strength are 10 and 10, and potential loss, aka stakes, is also 10. A character will be loved as a father figure—a hero to admire, as a child—a poor thing to be saved, or as a sibling—someone "just like me" to identify with.

2. **The outcome is in favor of the good.** During the course of the film, the protagonist must appear much weaker than the opponent, about to lose it all, but never losing completely. For a full cathartic experience, the protagonist should win with 10 over 0. During the course of the film, however, the protagonist can go as low as 1, while the antagonist must stay close to a 10, never going lower than the protagonist—lest that signal the end of the film prematurely. As soon as the protagonist wins over by a single point, the film is officially over in the mind of the viewer, and that must not happen until the very end. If it happens before—whatever happens afterwards must be cut out, with the exception of a breathing section to understand what just happened. This is the same concept of not overselling something: once the buyer is sold, stop selling, or they might start disliking the product.

3. **Good and evil.** The protagonist, who symbolizes the good, and the antagonist, who symbolizes the evil, must be fighting against each other, otherwise there is no problem, and there is no

story. However, each one of them must possess both good and evil traits, in order to complicate and enrich the story. Within each one of them, the ratio of good and evil can be also high, as in 10 to 9 of good in a protagonist, and 10 to 9 of evil in the antagonist. If either of them is clearly good or bad, with ratios such as 10 to 1, for example, the story becomes less interesting to the viewer.

Expressionism and Impressionism.

For me, there is a clear association between German Expressionism and horror, and French Impressionism—and psychological thrillers. Expressionism makes us look and react, and Impressionism makes us look and imagine. The feeling in Expressionism flows from the image to the viewer, and in Impressionism—from the viewer to the image. Impressionism images look inward, and take us along with them. Expressionist images look at us, and, with a stark eye contact, wait for a reaction.

What is a film genre?

A genre is a goal with a set of rules. A goal is how the film must make the viewer feel, and the rules are how the film can go about it. Whatever feeling dominates the film determines its genre, however every genre contains all possible genres, but in different degrees. Be it comedy, drama, thriller, or horror,—they all contain something of every other genre that there is, just like white contains all possible colors. No comedy is pure comedy, without any dramatic notes. Mystery overtones are always present, even if in tiniest doses. All of horror will have something, if only slightly, funny in it. Horror is fear, comedy is laughter, drama is empathy, mystery is excitement: all those are present in all films, no matter the genre.

It would be helpful to set up a chart for every film, with an estimation of how much of each genre is present in it. That could actually translated into color value, if each genre were to have its own.

FINE ARTS

"The most beautiful thing in the world is a beautiful idea,"—said Mr. Reed Wright.

Classical vs modern art.

Classical art is about what I see and feel, modern art is about what I think and imagine. Modern art heavily derives its meaning from its context. Classical art meaning endures, as long as human nature remains unchanged.

Extract of a person.

If you were to freshly squeeze someone into a juice, if you were able to extract their essential oil, it would come out as their handwriting, drawing, and painting.

Synesthetic colors and tastes.

In my mind, sweet is pink, bitter is black, sour is yellow, salty is white. Mixing colors is like cooking.

Flowers and leaves.

An image consists of leaves and flowers, just like a ring consists of a frame and a stone. Flowers are the focus, the peak experience, leaves are the background. Many artistic images are just a bunch of leaves, and that is why are they are mediocre, vapid, and uninteresting.

When art is alive.

Some works of art are like cadavers with makeup on them—they are dead. They don't give us a reason to engage, because there is no one alive beyond the surface. Or worse—that person is mentally ill. In either case, there is no story for us to listen and give our heart to.

Vectors and equilibrium.

For every work of art, one can assess balance in composition, color, and light, by adding up the values found throughout each of them. Every value can be expressed as a vector, pointing in a certain direction, and then one can add them all up. That kind of calculation measure quality in art objects, without its being explicitly available. When the sum it does not add up to a zero, then a work of art is perceived as unfinished or ill-conceived, or ill-executed.

There is another measure of quality in art: consistency of design. It is all about how well the work follows its apparent rules. If it follows them consistently, then it is esteemed higher. If the rules are not evident because they are confusing, the work is dismissed as inferior. Even in a painting that is partially in the tradition of cubism, and partially—pointillism, there is a rule that allows two separate styles, and then one watches for the interaction between them. It has to be clear, otherwise—the intent is either not there, or one must try harder to understand what it is.

So, for example, one would not be constructing a building that is half Baroque and half Bauhaus, unless that was deliberate. Not noticing the inconsistency is inconceivable. If the inconsistency is haphazard, the work will be downgraded. However, if the fusion of two styles is uniform throughout the structure, then it is esteemed higher.

Makeup: coverup vs decoration.

There are two opposing tendencies in the tradition of body adornment and makeup. They differ in their goals: one is aims at covering up and distorting the underlying body, and the other one—to enhance and decorate what is already there.

The developed world, and the West, seem to follow the cover-up tradition. The examples are numerous. One major one is makeup: cover up sticks, cover up foundations, plastic surgery, etc. All the tools of cover-up traditions are geared toward concealing the truth. Only in this tradition one will find decorations with front and back side. For example, stud earrings in the West will have a pretty side on the front, and the ugly clasp on the back—as if no one will see it. In the West, the dichotomy between the visible and concealed sides is symbolic of hypocrisy and fragility of structure. One cannot glance behind the ear, in order to avoid the unaesthetic side, but the side is till there. And, this knowledge of its existence spoils the aesthetic experience, at least, for me. It is the same with clothes: less expensive items in the West have unfinished unsightly edges on the inside, which expose themselves every time someone removes that article. The more expensive ones will have lining that will beautify the inner walls of a garment.

In the East and also in the primitive cultures, self-decoration and clothing items appear to be complete and rounded, in a sense that they don't have the front to show off and a back to conceal. They also do not aim at distorting the human nature, but aim to emphasize, enhance, and add to it. The earrings are usually hoops that are beautiful, all the way around, hiding nothing. They tend to have a rounded backside that is does not hurt the skin, if the ear is pressed, and are aesthetically pleasing, often having its own design. Clothes are equally decorated from the outside and the inside. Makeup does not cover anything, but enhances what is underneath. Face painting all over the primitive cultures are a testament. Even the Japanese geishas have a piece of their otherwise painted neck—exposed, so as to pay its respects to the flesh underneath the heavy white paint. In such cultures, costumes don't have pads to create an illusion of wider shoulders, or fluffier skirts—for larger behinds, as they do in the West. Every shape and form is considered beautiful, in that it is not altered but emphasized, and with this emphasis, what might seem as a defect in the West, becomes a new aesthetic standard.

Genre vs rules.

When giving their opinion on a work of art, people will often comment on their like or dislike of the genre, disregarding the quality of the execution. Is this a dilution affect? A genre is just a set of rules, a set of challenges, a game that an artist plays, and the outcome is the work of art that is then judged. It must be judged according to the rules of that genre, just like a winner in a chess game must be judged according to the rules of chess, and not checkers. A film should never be judged based on its belonging to a certain genre: one can dislike a genre, but not the film, simply because it belongs to it.

A mental experiment.

You can check your imagination by watching a video with your eyes closed, and ears wide-open, and see what your mind imagines, as it hears the soundtrack. Then, go back to the same episode, and watch it with your eyes open. Did you imagine much greater and impressive things, with more detail? Then, your imagination is wild-at-heart!

SCIENCE AS ART

"All of art is science, except those parts that we still don't understand—-we call those art,"—thought Mr. Reed Wright.

Why is science so often considered superior to art? It could be a reflection of our moral values. The ultimate goal of science is to find the truth.   The ultimate goal of art is to find pleasure. In addition, science can explain art, but art can only describe science, evaluating its pleasure value. An artistic pursuit can, unbeknownst to itself, lead to scientific truth, but it does not seek the same truth or in the same way that science does, nor for the same reason. Art can enjoy everything, and science can understand everything.

Yet, if we compare art and science on the level of transcendence they can cause a human to experience, we will find that they are absolutely equal. Some will even argue art is far superior to science in its ability to elevate the human spirit.

How is science an art?

If the art's goal is aesthetic pleasure, a scientific pursuit can also be experienced as that. Scientific insights and even mere observations can cause a dedicated scientist to experience an extreme aesthetic pleasure. Even seeing the speed of light reflected everywhere—in how fast a water drop will fall, in how fast the sound of thunder reaches your ears, and trickles down to the cellular processes that determine how fast we age,—can be deeply aesthetically pleasing. The speed of everything is tuned to a certain measure, and its range regresses to a single setting—the radio station of God.

Really, any epiphany in science is necessarily an aesthetic experience. The beauty of ideas, patterns, and mental combinations can be much more intense than any visual or auditory aesthetic experience, and is akin to experiencing passionate love for another person. In fact, humans tend to anthropomorphize all abstract concepts, and even physical objects, so that they can relate to them.

Understanding calculus for the first time, seeing how an egg is being fertilized, witnessing a chemical release of gas, after mixing two liquids, comparing galaxies to the organization of neurons in the brain—they are all deep aesthetic experiences.

Repeating patterns in nature are another example. The outline of a flower's petals follow the same pattern as the outline of mountains, seen from the bird's eye view, and the same patterns as the outline of a human hair under a microscope. The scales are drastically removed from each other, but the patterns are stunningly similar!

MUSIC

"The whole world is asound with music!"—exclaimed Mr. Reed Wright.

When taking a shower, listen to the drone that the stream of water makes. There is a dominant note, and there is a chord around it. You can sing in harmony with it, and you will feel grounded, one with the spirit of water, through its music. It is the same with the natural streams and waterfalls, with the desert wind, trees, plants, animals, people, and places around the world: they all sound like complex chords, and listening to their notes the way we listen to a symphony can become an experience of transcendence.

Major vs minor chords.

Music gives me visual sensations: musical chords look like overlapping waves, like wavy threads woven together. Some are tighter than others, and when the waves overlap, they make this trilling sound, like a micro vibrato that gives each sound its overall timber. When the waves are perfectly overlapping each other, we get very clean chords that sound in unison and don't irritate us emotionally. They feel happy, and we call them major. When the waves are just a bit shifted, giving them a difference of one tone or less, then the sound is quite disturbing. The chord of Devil's Fourth is named after devil precisely for the horrifying emotion its makes us experience. As the overlap shifts a little more, we get a minor chord, which sounds sad to us, being little less alarming and disturbing to the brain.

A little shift sounds terrifying (half or whole tone), a little more shift sounds sad (minor third), then it is a happier chord again (major third), then a slightly sadder chord (fourth), then back to terrifying Devil's fourth, then coming back to major fifth. It is unison, to terrifying, to minor, to major, to minor, to terrifying, to major again. Even this pattern looks like a wave.

Minor and more cacophonous chords literally make our brain experience pain. The terrifying chords are the ones that cause most pain, so we process them as danger, and our fight-or-flight response is activated. Minor chords cause us less pain, so we feel sadness. Major chords sound happy to us because they give us a little disturbance: just enough to perk us up, and incite a release of endorphins. Complete overlap of notes is very soothing: it is neither saddening, nor stimulating.

In fact, there is no such a thing a complete overlap of sound in nature, since there is no clean sound with only one wave to it. All sounds are a combination of various waves, which gives them that natural quality and particular timber. When humans are exposed to electronically engineered sounds that are as clean as can be, they actually respond negatively: the brain is disturbed with a sterile sound that lacks the richness and fulness of timber brain is used to.

Pure voices.

Just like there are no completely pure sounds in nature, there are also no pure voices. Each style of music imbues a voice with a particular "accent"—a particular style of timber, vibrato, and intonation. For example, many types of vibrato appropriate in jazz would be completely unacceptable in opera. Opera is considered a classic style of singing, with the purest voices, but even there, the projection necessary tends to prevent all but the very best from keeping their sound bell-like, light, and unburdened by sound intruders, arising from the body's trying to make the sound louder.

Not many people are able appreciate opera. To some, operatic voice forever sound like a caricature. For them, it is a never acquired taste of the accent that that musical genre overlays on the voice. For others, liking it is almost instantaneous, because for them the voice comes along with a beautiful melody, beautiful harmony, beautiful people, set design, and the story. Yet others consider operatic singing the purest and the most aesthetically pleasing form of sound that a human can produce.

DESIGN

"Your limitations are your inspirations, and your best credential is your confidence level"—said Mr. Reed Wright.

Despite its illusiveness, creativity in design can be measured in many ways, one of which is what I call Technology Utility Ratio: the total utility of a gadget over the user effort needed to operate it. The bigger it is, the better the gadget: usefulness must be maximized, and user effort—minimized. The more creative a designer, the bigger the ratio.

Method vs insight.

In an individualistic culture, it is harder to develop empathy than in a group-oriented society. Designers in individualist-oriented societies rely on methodology. In addition, when people come into design from the technology side, as opposed to the "human" side, such as psychology or other humanistic field, they tend to focus on methods as being crucial in understanding what the humans need in the design.

They tend to design ever-increasingly sophisticated methods of assessing the humans, mostly quantitative. They use methods as a crutch and a substitute to the good old empathetic synthesis and analysis. Instead of simplifying what is observed, they can slip into making it look more complex by piling their convoluted methodology and documentation, and heaps of uninterpreted data on their cases. The little insight that comes out of all of this mess is predictably lacking in relevance, and is then, like a snowball, is fed into the algorithms and assumptions to be used for further studies, they create propagated error. It just looks like they are building a tower of Babylon that is certainly bound to crumble. The priority to quantify all insight produces a false sense of assurance of being closer to the truth, and an impossible way of validating one's research.

A meaningful insight is only possible through empathy, and in group societies, where empathy is highly valued, insight comes naturally. In individualist societies, learning empathy, so that it really makes you feel differently, and not just think differently about other human beings, is the solution to this problem. If at all possible.

Affordance.

Affordance is a physical property of a product that tells the user how the product should be used. If you see a handle, you naturally lean to grab it, if you see a dial, you automatically turn it around. A curious case in anthropology is where perceived affordance of an object allows the scientists to reconstruct how the object was used thousands of years ago. So, if something has a handle, it is highly likely that it was used the way is most convenient for human hands.

Sapir-Whorf Hypothesis and influence.

Design of any product directs and influences how people think, just like language does according to Sapir-Whorf Hypothesis. The buttons and navigation tools force the user to take the paths that are available to us, and we can only click the buttons that are available. It does not completely stop us from thinking and feeling what we want, but cumulatively, guides and reinforces certain ways of thinking and doing things. Essentially, your natural thought is discouraged, discriminated against, and subdued through repetition, and redirected by the paths provided by the design of products we use. Designers play God—that is how much power they have over us, who we are, and whom we will become.

What is your User Experience value?

What is your personal UX value? As a parent, friends, employee, UX designer. All those are roles we play in our lives that serve as tools in the hands and minds of others around us. Are we functional, usable, and pleasurable to deal with?

Do you scale as a person? As a lover, as an employee? Is your positive attitude conditional, or is it freely given out, once a positive relationship is established? As an employee, do you need constant surveillance and direction to keep you motivated, or do you hear an idea once and go away to work independently and without a need to constantly micro-manage you?

Just something to think about.

User Experience of teaching.

Teachers are essentially UX designers. The lessons have to be functional (produce a result of understanding), usable (easy to understand and apply), and delightful (fun and inspirational). Moreover, good teachers are Agile UX'ers— they quickly change their techniques according to the student's reaction, until they get the right result. It is really quick trial and error—what a rat naturally does to get out of a labyrinth.

Creativity in design.

Creativity is a mindset of peace and goodness a designer must maintain, even in the midst of outright negativity and utilitarianism. Design is not about being the best. It is not about being the winner, the star, the richest, or the most famous. When all those fake and noxious values disappear, people start feeling free, happy and creative. It's the lightness that you feel at the moment when you let those constraints go that instantly that turns you into a free thinker, and a wild creative.

LEARNING

"I have learned how much I still don't know, but how will I ever know what it is?"—thought to himself Mr. Reed Wright.

Einstein didn't have a computer, Aristotle didn't have a Ph.D., and Leonardo Da Vinci did not have an MFA. It is not the degrees in your studies, but it is the studies in your degrees that matter. The most important for creativity is not technical knowledge, but an education in the liberal arts, where one learns how to feel and think, where one develops one's taste and intuition. Someone with technical knowledge and no liberal arts education is like an AI machine gone rogue!

We are all more creative than we know it. It is just that our brain hides it from us, so that we wouldn't go insane. We can only go insane if our intellectual ability is not up to par with our creative energy. If our intellectual ability is not high enough, our brain will not allow into our consciousness much of what it perceives on the background, just to keep us mentally together.

So that we can handle our creative potential, we need to train and develop our brain muscle—our intellectual capacity. The combination of mathematics, music, and literature is a magic trinity of training tools that will cause your brain to literally grow what it takes to support intense creativity.

The arc of competence.

Growing one's intellectual capacity to support creativity happens in stages: unawareness, sharp awareness, and then back to unawareness of the structure and logic of your creative material.

At first, one is not aware of the beauty, the details, the sense, and what is going on overall—in any art and science. One does not know the rules, and if one does—one has a hard time following along. This is the stage of ignorant bliss, or curious oblivion, where one may or may not be aware of what they are missing. This describes everyone in at least one category of human knowledge. Even a medical surgery can be seen as art, and most of us will have no idea what is being done, if we watch it happen. At this stage, creativity simply does not have any platform on which to develop.

The second stage in gaining competence is becoming adroit with the rules of the game: it could be chess, or it could be modern art, it is all the same. At this stage, one's intellectual capacity is being trained, while creativity is still limited, being tethered down by one's close attention to the rules. An example is when one has to follow meticulously the rules of how to write a good story, making sure that nothing is left out, and is too busy and weary of deviating from the sure course to let their imagination run wild.

The third stage is when creativity is finally unleashed, and is fully supported by one's intellectual capacity. The rules and structure have now become automatic, and need no close monitoring. An example is when someone paints a painting, without thinking of what brush to use and of how composition and perspective work: they simply paint. It is in this stage when our subconscious is most closely connected to our artistic execution, and when our creativity is at its peak. At this stage, bringing up to consciousness what is intuitively felt and understood can be harmful to our creative process.

Once we reach this stage, we can feel the magic bliss of creativity that everyone dreams about.